KEEPING THE
TEN COMMA...

Written by Carol Ann Morrow
Illustrated by Miguel D. Lopez
ISBN 1-936020-17-1

Artwork and Text © 2011 Aquinas Kids, Phoenix, Arizona.

Moses is the great leader who received the Commandments from God on Mount Sinai.

The First Commandment: **"I, the Lord, am your God. You shall not have other gods besides Me."**

DON'T:
You will not love anything or anyone more than you love God.

DO:
Your actions will show that God is more important to you than presents or parties or games.

The Second Commandment: **"You shall not take the name of the LORD your God in vain."**

6

DON'T:
You will not say "Oh my God" in a disrespectful or careless way.

DO:
When you speak of God, it will always be with love.

The Third Commandment: **"Remember to keep holy the Sabbath day."**

DON'T:
You will not misbehave at Mass.

DO:
You will put God first in what you choose to do on Sundays.

The Fourth Commandment: "Honor your father and your mother."

12

DON'T:
You will not disrespect or disobey your parents.

13

DO:
You will show your love for them in what you say and DO.

The Fifth Commandment: **"You shall not kill."**

DON'T:
You will never threaten to hurt someone.

DO:
You will treat all living things with kindness.

The Sixth Commandment: "You shall not commit adultery."

DON'T:
God wants us to keep ourselves pure, because we belong to Him. Do not watch shows where marriage doesn't seem important.

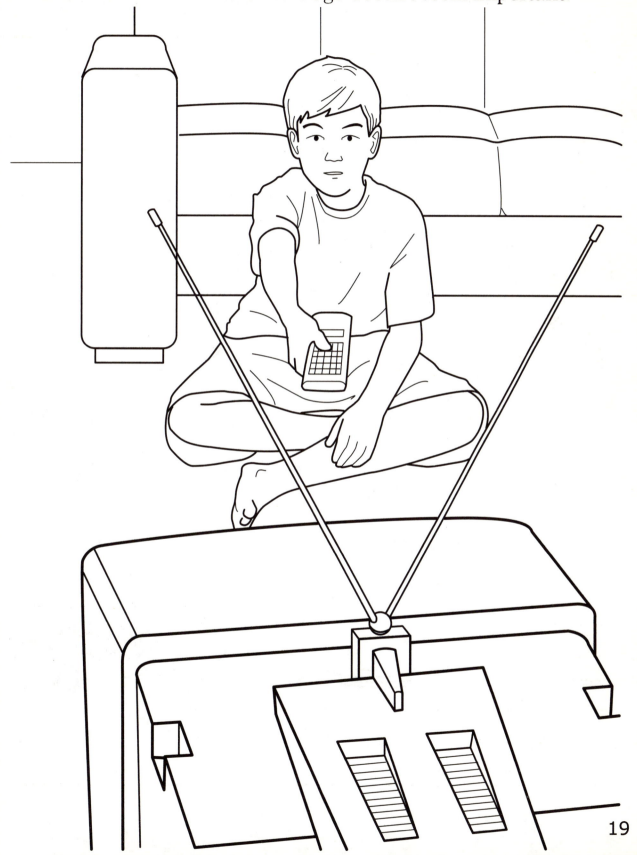

DO:
Fathers and mothers who love each other and obey God keep themselves for each other. They do not give their special love to anyone else.

The Seventh Commandment: "You shall not steal."

21

DON'T:
You will not take anything that belongs to someone else.

DO:
You will share the things that belong to you—just as God has shared everything with you.

The Eighth Commandment: **"You shall not bear false (dishonest) witness against your neighbor."**

DON'T:
You will not tell lies about what you have done.

DO:
You will speak the truth whenever you are asked questions.

The Ninth Commandment: **"You shall not covet your neighbor's wife."**

DON'T:
You will not think of other people's families as better than your own.

DO:
You can choose to be happy in your own family, with your own parents, just as they are.

The Tenth Commandment: **"You shall not covet your neighbor's goods."**

DON'T:
You will not resent it if your friend gets something you would like to have.

31

DO:
You will be happy for your friends when they get gifts that you also like.